This book belongs to :

_____

_____

_____

Copyright © 2023 All rights reserved.
No part of this book may be reproduced or transmitted in any form or by any means, electronic or mechanical, including photocopying, recording, or by any information storage and retrieval system, without permission in writing from the publisher.
This book is a work of fiction
. Names, characters, places, and incidents
either are products of the author's imagination
or are used fictitiously. Any resemblance to actual events or locales or persons, living or dead, is entirely coincidental.

COLOR TEST